The Connecticut Guide to Nursing Home Abuse

By:
Attorney Jay Ruane
Attorney Jill Ruane

Edited by:
Jennifer Sanfilippo

For permission requests, write to the address below.

Designed and published by:

Different Middle Initial, LLC.

1 Enterprise Drive

Shelton, CT, 06484

TABLE OF CONTENTS

FORWARD

The process of growing older can be difficult. As a child, it can be painful to watch your parent get older and slowly need more and more assistance. It might start with something simple, such as your father needing help cutting the lawn or your mother losing her ability to safely drive her car. But soon, you might notice that your parent is having trouble with everyday tasks, such as dressing him or herself, eating, and walking. As these issues become more prominent, you will have some tough decisions to make.

If having your parent live with you or another family member is not an option, there are other living situations that you can pursue. For many elderly people, moving into a nursing home will provide them with the treatment and attentive care that they need. This can be an excellent option for your family. However, it is imperative that you do not make this decision lightly. Finding the right nursing home can mean the difference between happiness and misery for your mother or father.

Not all nursing homes are created equally. If you are beginning the search for a nursing home for your parent, or if you have just gone through this process, you know this statement to be true. We have created this book to help you navigate this process and find a good nursing home for your loved ones. Some nursing homes are understaffed and do not provide the treatment that is necessary for their residents. In recent years, nursing home neglect and abuse have exploded. We have dealt with cases where nursing home residents have faced physical, emotional, sexual, and financial abuse. A combination of many factors has caused the nursing home abuse that we see our clients face today, and we will discuss these factors in this book. In addition, we will show you how to find a safe nursing home for your parent. If you've already found a nursing home, this book will teach you how to stay vigilant and keep an eye out for incidents of neglect or abuse.

There are no guarantees that your mother or father will be treated with respect in a nursing home, but by following the tips in this book, you can weed out neglectful institutions and do everything in your power to ensure that your parent has a positive nursing home experience. Even once you find a nursing home, you need to actively monitor your parent's living arrangements to ensure that he or she is properly cared for. Even homes that seem great at first can start showing signs of neglect or abuse under new management, with new employees, or simply as time goes by.

We got together to write this book because each of us brings important information that you need to the table. Together, we can explain all of the medical and legal issues that you need to be aware of as you develop a relationship with a nursing home. Our knowledge and unique perspectives have culminated in the creation of this book. Here, we share all of our tips of the trade in the hopes that by following these suggestions, you can minimize the possibility of having a loved one experience abuse in a nursing home.

If you suspect that a loved one has been abused in a nursing home, now is the time to act. Contact a lawyer today to begin minimizing the damage and to make sure that the perpetrator(s) are apprehended. You can contact us at 203-925-9200 to discuss your situation during a free consultation. We are happy to guide you and your family through this process and help you heal from this experience.

INTRODUCTION

What is Abuse?

There are many different types of abuse that people - especially nursing home residents - can experience. In nursing homes, common forms of abuse include:

- Physical abuse
- Sexual abuse
- Emotional/psychological abuse
- Neglect
- Financial abuse
- Healthcare fraud
- Insurance fraud
- Medical errors

Physical abuse is defined as any unwanted and intentional physical contact. Common examples of physical abuse in nursing homes include: hitting, punching, and any other physical injuries.

Sexual abuse is any unwanted and intentional sexual contact, whether this is between a resident and a staff member or two residents. This includes sexual assault, unwanted touching, coerced nudity, sodomy, and more.

Emotional and psychological abuse is an intentional act that is meant to reduce a person's self-esteem and self-worth. Common forms of emotional abuse in nursing homes include: screaming, insulting the resident, intimidation, humiliation, isolation, etc.

Neglect occurs when the staff in a nursing home fails to provide basic needs for a resident, such as personal hygiene, food, shelter, clothing, water, medicine, etc.

Financial abuse is a very common type of abuse that the elderly face. This can occur when someone takes advantage of an elderly person's financial situation. This can include forging a signature, stealing possessions, coercing someone into signing a contract or financial document, cashing checks without permission, etc. Another common form of financial abuse is healthcare fraud, which many elderly people go through when they are in a nursing home.

Healthcare fraud occurs when someone files dishonest or false health care claims so that they can profit from the claims.

Insurance fraud is defined by an action that intends to defraud a person or a company through some form of insurance process.

Medical errors are any negative effects of health care that could have been prevented. For example, any inaccurate treatment or diagnosis could be considered a medical error.

Discrimination is defined as unfair treatment of a person based on a category that he or she falls into. For example, people can be discriminated against based on their race, gender, disability, age, etc.

Can it Happen to My Parent?

You will be shocked by the prevalence of abuse that occurs in nursing homes. While many abuse cases go unreported, statistics show that at least one in three nursing home residents will experience some form of abuse during their residency. Female residents with specific disabilities or special needs tend to be abused more than other elderly residents. In addition, non-white nursing home residents generally experience more abuse than white residents.

Nursing Home Abuse Factors

Many factors combine to cause abuse in nursing homes. Some common factors that lead to abuse are:

- **Ageism/social stigma**. Some people feel that the elderly, especially those who are disabled or who have special needs, are not normal people. Unlike in countries such as Japan, the elderly in the U.S. are not as revered and respected. This makes it easy for people to justify mistreating the elderly.

- **Opportunity**. There is a lot of opportunity to abuse the elderly in different ways. Those with dementia are victims of various forms of abuse because assailants know that they will not remember the abuse. Confused and dependent elderly residents often do not realize when they are being taken advantage of financially, which encourages some staff members to commit financial crimes.

- **Job stressors**. Many nursing home staff members are overworked and underpaid. They work long shifts and deal with frustrating situations every day. The baby boomer generation has led to an explosion in the elderly population. Many nursing homes are not ready to deal with the increase in residents, leading to overcrowded homes and procedures that are difficult to scale. All of these factors can make nurses and other staff members lose their tempers and act in ways that they normally wouldn't act. This is certainly no excuse, but it is the cause of many abuse cases.

- **Education**. A lack of education on how to properly treat residents and lack of continued education on the subject can result in unintended injuries to residents.

These are some of the most common factors that have increased nursing home neglect and abuse in recent years. We know that the potential of abuse is not a risk you are willing to take when it comes to your parents. You can learn how to protect them from such neglect and abuse by following the steps in this book.

RESEARCHING THE NURSING HOME

When you determine that it is in your parent's best interest to put him or her in a nursing home, your first step is to research several different facilities in your area. The initial research will weed out homes that do not fit your parent's needs, homes that do not have room for more residents, places that are too expensive, and homes that you simply do not feel comfortable with. This list is designed to help you find the right nursing home.

Even if you already chose a nursing home, please review this list of potential risk factors to ensure that your parent is currently living in a safe and caring environment, free from neglect and abuse.

1. Determine if a Nursing Home is Right for Your Parent

There are many different assistance options that you can pursue if you find that you can no longer take care of your parent on your own. While a nursing home is a very common option, and it is the right option for certain situations, there are alternative treatment opportunities that you should consider before settling on a nursing home. One of these other options might be best for your parent. Consider the following alternatives to a nursing home.

Home health aide: Home health aides work in an elderly person's home, helping with everyday tasks such as walking, dressing, bathing, etc. A home health aide can also cook, clean, and arrange transportation for an elderly client. Some home health aides are even certified to help with medical issues. Home health aides do not provide live-in assistance, but they can spend a good portion of the day helping their elderly clients fulfill day-to-day tasks.

Live in assistance: A live in assistant is similar to a home health aide, but one major difference is that he or she does not simply visit the elderly client. Assistance is provided 24 hours a day, usually by a team of nurses who take shifts with your parent.

Adult day care: This non-residential facility will meet an elderly person's social, physical, and emotional needs during the day.

Respite care: Respite care is provided to relieve everyday caregivers of their duties. This is a temporary institutional care option.

Continued care retirement community: This option is for elderly people who can and wish to maintain their independence while receiving necessary assistance from nurses and caregivers. In a continued care retirement community, residents can live independently in homes or apartments, but they will receive treatment and assistance when needed.

These options are just a few alternatives to nursing homes that you and your loved one should consider before making the decision to find a nursing home.

2. Ask for Referrals

Trusting strangers with the care of one of the most important people in your life can be difficult. For this reason, many people choose to ask trusted friends, family members, and colleagues about their experiences with nursing homes. Oftentimes, a loved one is going through a situation that is similar to yours, and he or she can give you some advice. Your parent might even have some friends in a nursing home that he or she is interested in living in. Instead of blindly hoping that a nursing home you choose will treat your parent with respect, you can ask loved ones about their experiences with nursing homes. A good recommendation from a person that you trust can be a great place to start in your nursing home search.

3. Understand Your Loved One's Personal Needs

First, identify your parent or loved one's needs. Not all nursing homes are equipped to handle every person's need or medical concern. You need to communicate with your mom or dad to fully understand common issues such as:

- Dietary restrictions
- Current prescribed medication
- Specialty doctor appointments
- Physical limitations
- Mental limitations
- Physical therapy needs
- Grief over the loss of a spouse or loved one
- Depression

- Emotional needs
- Assistance walking, dressing, bathing, using the bathroom, eating, etc.
- Loss of memory/dementia

Discussing your parent's needs can be difficult. You may be unaware of the true extent of your parent's current limitations, and discussing his or her needs can be shocking to you. This is very common, as some elderly people do not want to burden family members with their problems, or they feel embarrassed about their needs. Therefore, it is important to be gentle and supportive while discussing your parent's needs. Stressing the importance of honesty at this time will help you communicate with your parent and truly find a way to help him or her.

4. Find a Home That Fits Your Parent's Needs

While most nursing home facilities can handle the issues listed above and other common issues that elderly people face, there are some facilities that have limitations. For example, if your parent is suffering from Alzheimer's disease, and the nursing home facility and staff cannot meet needs related to this disease, you must find another nursing home that can.

You can contact a nursing home and ask them what types of special services they offer if you cannot find this information online. Identifying a nursing home's services is a critical step in choosing the appropriate nursing home for your loved one.

5. Understand Your Loved One's Financial Needs

When finding the right living situation for your parent, his or her physical and emotional needs are not the only needs that have to be considered. You should also think about how your parent will afford to live in a nursing home. If your parent has Medicare or Medicaid, this is a good start. Your parent can use one of these services to pay for his or her care. In addition, these services will protect your parent from discrimination, neglect, and abuse.

Another way to pay for nursing home care is through private finances. This might be an option depending on your parent and your family's personal situation. Again, you should have an open, honest discussion about your parent's finances as well as your own in an attempt to determine if private funds can pay for the nursing home. Understanding the financial situation will help you narrow down what nursing homes your parent can and cannot qualify for.

6. Determine the Nursing Home's Payment Policy

Just because your parent has Medicare or Medicaid does not necessarily mean that these programs will pay for the nursing home. In general, Medicare will not cover long-term nursing home care. In many cases, if your parent has Medicaid, this will pay for a nursing home or live-in care, but this is not always the case. Not every nursing home may participate in the Medicare or Medicaid program, so you should check the payment policy before you seriously consider a particular nursing home.

In general, choosing a nursing home that is certified with Medicaid or Medicare is in your parent's best interest. This is because, when you are a resident in a Medicaid or Medicare certified facility, federal and state law protect your rights. Such rights/protection for your parent include the right:

- To be treated with respect
- Not to be discriminated against
- To exercise his or her rights as a U.S. citizen
- To participate in program activities
- Not to be neglected, abused, or restrained
- To make complaints against the nursing home
- To have appropriate medical care
- To be given information regarding fees and services of the nursing home
- To manage his or her own money or having a trusted friend or family member manage it on his or her behalf
- To privacy for his or her personal property
- To see visitors
- To receive social services such as counseling
- To leave the nursing home
- To have a representative or family notified if he or she is injured or experiences a physical issue

7. Location

For many families, location is an essential part of finding a nursing home for their parents or loved ones. Finding a nursing home close to your home will ensure that you can visit your loved one at any time, for any reason. Whether you are concerned about the issue of medical emergencies, neglect, abuse, or if you just want to make sure that you can visit your parent regularly, finding a nursing home close to where you live will make this process much easier for your whole family. For these reasons, location is a factor that you should consider when discussing nursing home options with your family.

8. Availability

This is another basic factor that you should consider when trying to find a nursing home for your parent. Does the home have a room available for your parent? Is there a wait list for the home? If you think that you've found the perfect home, but there is a wait to get into it, you and your family will have to determine if waiting is a viable option, or if you should move on to another home.

9. Research the Home's History

Check to see if the nursing home has testimonials on its website from residents and family members of residents. You should also consider asking around to determine the general opinion of the nursing home. What does your parent's doctor think of the home? Do any of your friends, colleagues, or family members have experience with this home? Was the experience positive or negative? You should also consider previous complaints filed against the nursing home. Has there been a pattern of neglect and abusive behavior? Has the nursing home made an effort to address and fix any issues? These are all important questions that you should be asking as you research a nursing home. A nursing home's history can show you the direction that it is headed in.

10. Research the Home's History with the Police

You should consider the history that a nursing home you are looking at has with the police. Check to see if any reports have been filed for neglect and abuse against the home itself or staff members of the nursing home. This will give you as accurate an account as you can get regarding the history of neglect and abuse in the nursing home.

Another thing that you can look for when researching a nursing home is the criminal history of its staff members. While staff members in a nursing home may not be charged or convicted of neglect and abuse, you can check to see if these people have violent or antisocial pasts. If a staff member has previously been charged with a crime such as assault, he or she may be predisposed to abusing residents in the nursing home.

11. Contact an Ombudsman

An ombudsman is a person hired to investigate complaints. For our purposes, an ombudsman is an official who investigates neglect complaints, abuse complaints, and other complaints made against staff members of nursing homes or the nursing home itself. If you can get in touch with an ombudsman who investigated claims made against a nursing home you have been researching, you may be able to get even more information concerning neglect and abuse in that nursing home. This can help you make decisions regarding which nursing homes to avoid and which ones will be suitable for your parent.

12. Schedule a Visit

Once you researched different nursing homes and narrowed down your list, it is time to schedule on-site visits. Only by actually visiting the nursing home will you understand what the culture and environment of the home is truly like. Be sure to schedule a visit at each of the final nursing home options to conduct interviews, view the home, and more.

VISITING THE HOME: INFORMAL INTERVIEW

Visiting a nursing home is an essential step in determining whether or not it is a good fit for your parent. All nursing homes look good online, but up close and personal, you will be able to distinguish the good homes from the bad ones. In addition, it is important that you schedule an interview with a staff member such as a nurse, the nursing home director, or the Director of Operations. However, in addition to these interviews, there are many things that you should look for when you visit the nursing home. This informal examination of the nursing home can help you make a final decision.

13. Residents' Grooming and Appearance

You can learn a lot about the care residents receive without ever speaking to a staff member or a resident. You can learn about the staff members' abilities and their attitudes towards the residents by looking around the home. If the residents are well groomed and appropriately dressed for the season, the staff members are probably diligent, caring, and attentive. However, if the residents look unkempt, disheveled, or unhygienic, the staff may not be doing their job well. Check to see if men are shaved or have trimmed beards, and if women are wearing makeup or have their hair done. If physical appearance is overlooked, staff members may be overlooking other areas of care as well.

14. Residents' Physical Injuries

If you notice any physical injuries or issues when you see residents in a nursing home, this could be a warning sign that neglect or abuse is taking place. When passing residents in the hallway or walking by bedroom doors, look for residents that look exceptionally thin or malnourished. Also keep your eye out for cuts, bruises, swelling, and other physical injuries that are easily visible. Of course, not all injuries are the result of abuse, but taking this factor into consideration when you make your final decision can help you choose the right nursing home.

15. Residents' Demeanor

Again, there are many reasons why residents that you visit might seem unhappy. Some may be dealing with serious depression or other mental illnesses. Others might just be having a bad day. But taking note of residents' demeanors when you visit a nursing home can help you determine the general environment in the facility that you are visiting. Do the residents seem happy? Are they friendly and greet you as you pass them in the hallways? Are they smiling? Or do they seem reserved, frightened, angry, or antisocial? A poor environment and culture in the nursing home can lead to this behavior. At the very least, you don't want your parent to live with a group of people who seem hostile or grumpy. At worst, you don't want them to be in a situation where they are fearful for their safety.

16. Personal Belongings

When you tour personal rooms, you should look for signs of personalization, which can help residents acclimate to living in a nursing home. Is it clear that residents may keep personal belongings with them? Is there space in closets, drawers, and their rooms to store personal items? While this is a small detail, personal items can be very comforting to elderly people who can no longer take care of themselves or visit with family and friends whenever they please. Having a photo album, personal clothing, or a favorite book with them can make this transition and experience easier for them. Make sure that residents are allowed to keep personal belongings with them in the nursing home that you are considering.

17. Privacy and Safety

Some personal belongings are valuable. Whether keeping expensive jewelry or sensitive financial information with them, elderly people have a right to keep their personal property locked up for safety reasons. When you view rooms, do you see lockable cabinets or closets where elderly people can store their valuables? Do residents have access to safes where they can put sensitive material? In order to feel safe and ensure that other residents and staff members do not steal from residents, they should have access to privacy for their possessions.

In addition to privacy for their property, residents should have access to privacy for themselves. Make sure that there are private or semi-private rooms available in the nursing home, and that private bathrooms are an option. The right to privacy of person is another right that all nursing home residents should have.

18. Comfort and Communication

When touring rooms in a nursing home, make note of the items in each room. Are there telephones in each room, or are residents allowed to keep cell phones on them? Are there televisions in each room? Do the rooms have WiFi? Is there a computer center, or individual computers in each room? These are all devices that residents will need for comfort. In addition, access to phones, wireless Internet, etc. will allow the residents to contact loved ones, whether to maintain relationships, or for emergency purposes. Easy access to communication will help your parent and you adjust to the nursing home and help you feel confident in the home.

19. Talk with Residents

While observing is a great way to learn the truth about a nursing home, talking with residents can clear up some confusion and tell you a lot about the home itself. If possible, you should seriously consider talking with at least one resident while you're visiting, even if it is only for a few minutes. Consider asking questions such as:

- How long have you been living here?
- How often do you visit with your family?
- Do you like living here? Why? Why not?
- What is the best part of living here?
- What is the worst thing about living here?
- How does the staff treat you?

These are just a few basic questions that you can start with when talking to residents. Pay attention to not only what their answers are, but *how* they answer. Do they avoid eye contact when singing the home's praises? Do they look around nervously before answering questions? Read the resident's body language to determine if the resident is lying to you out of fear or telling you the truth.

You should also take what residents say with a grain of salt. Residents might be nitpicking about the home or they might not be mentally stable enough to give you legitimate answers. Go with your instincts and don't assume the worst when talking with residents.

20. Cleanliness

Use all of your senses when you are visiting a nursing home and trying to determine cleanliness. Especially consider what you see and what you smell.

Sight. What do you see? Is there dust all over the place, messes on the floor that have not been cleaned, and untidy rooms? Or is it clear that the nursing home keeps up with cleaning?

Smell. Does the nursing home have an overall clean smell, or are there unpleasant odors, such as rotting food or bodily function accidents that have not been cleaned up after? When you walk into a bedroom, does the odor get worse, as if bed sheets have not been changed?

The cleanliness of the nursing home that you choose is important. You don't want your loved one living in filth or dealing with unpleasant odors.

21. Smoking

A common safety issue in many buildings is smoking. You should check to make sure that there is a smoking policy in place in the nursing home that you are visiting. This policy should establish clear smoking and non-smoking areas in order to protect residents who are using oxygen tanks and who cannot be exposed to cigarettes for other reasons. In addition, keep your eyes out for smoke detectors in the nursing home, particularly in individual bedrooms. These precautionary measures can protect your parent from fires and other smoking incidents should he or she decide to live in that nursing home.

22. Windows

One aspect of making sure that all patients are comfortable is having a window in each bedroom. All residents should have access to fresh air, sunshine, and the positive benefits that go along with these privileges. If your loved one is assigned a room with no window, the room will not feel very homey. Your parent might feel more like a prisoner than a resident if he or she does not have consistent access to the outdoors. This is an extremely subtle yet important thing to look for when visiting nursing homes. Having a window in each bedroom is a simple way to boost morale and make your loved one feel comfortable at the nursing home.

23. Wheelchair Accessibility

Particularly if your mother or father uses a wheelchair or cane, it is important to make sure that the nursing home you are considering is wheelchair accessible. While this might seem like a no-brainer for a home that is catering to elderly people, you will be surprised at how many nursing homes have been slow to implement wheelchair accessibility. Check to make sure that there are wheelchair accessible bathrooms and bedrooms in the facilities before deciding on the nursing home. You should also make sure that the home has handrails in appropriate places, such as hallways, bathrooms, bathtubs, bedrooms, etc.

24. Noise Level

While you are in the home, what kind of noise levels do you notice? Is the place loud in general, with residents and staff members making a lot of noise? Even if this is the case, are there quiet places where residents can go to be alone with their thoughts? Are there quiet places where residents can meet with visitors, such as friends and family members? You should definitely look for a nursing home that is not too loud or frightening, so be alert to the kind of noises that you hear. Also consider the types of noises that you hear. Are they happy noises, such as residents partaking in fun activities and staff members whistling or singing? Or are they frightening noises, such as arguments between staff members and residents, or residents resisting treatment or assistance from nurses? Understanding the noise level and the types of noises that you hear in the nursing home can help you decide if this is the right nursing home for your parent or if it is not.

25. Staff-Resident Interaction

One very important observation that you should make while you are checking out a potential nursing home for your parent is the staff's relationship with and demeanor toward the residents. In most cases, you won't be able to shadow a staff member as he or she works with patients, and doing so may not teach you much, as the staff member will be on his or her best behavior if he or she knows that you're watching. However, if you happen to see any interactions between staff and residents, take note of them. Consider:

- How the staff members speak to the residents.
- How the staff members act towards the residents (ex. are they abrasive or rough with residents when providing treatment?).
- What is their body language like? Do staff members smile and speak kindly to residents, or do they avoid eye contact and speak in harsh tones?
- Do staff members seem frustrated, tired, or overworked?
- Do you notice any staff members raising their voices at residents?
- Are staff members complaining about their duties?
- Do staff members act recklessly when dealing with residents?
- Are staff members trying to connect with residents on a personal level? Do they ask about the resident's family or interests?
- Are derogatory comments made toward residents?
- How to the residents respond to the staff members? Do they seem happy to see them, or are they cold toward the staff?

By observing how staff members work with residents, you will get a good idea of the environment in the nursing home and how your parent would be treated should he or she become a resident in the nursing home.

26. Staff Interaction

Another important aspect of the nursing home that you should take note of when you are visiting is how the staff members interact with one another. Try to focus on staff interaction and think about how it appears to the average person walking through. Do staff members seem on edge when talking to one another? Do registered nurses or those in positions of power seem condescending to other staff members? Or are they patient and kind? Are staff members quick to jump down one another's throats, or do they try to work together to solve problems, cover shifts, and make the workplace a pleasant place to be? These factors will affect your parent while he or she is living at the nursing home. Making sure that staff members interact well with their colleagues is in your parent's best interest.

27. Outdoor Spaces

When you visit the facilities, take note of the outdoor space around the nursing home. Do you notice elderly people utilizing this space in some way? When choosing a nursing home, you want to make sure that your parent will have ample access to the outdoors. Make sure you take note of elderly people partaking in outdoor activities such as:

- Going for a walk
- Gardening
- Fishing
- Reading by a lake
- Organized activities, such as yoga, golf, etc.

- Yard games such as bocce, croquet, shuffleboard, etc.

Staying active will help your parent stay both physically and mentally healthy. Outdoor activities can bring great happiness to those living in a nursing home, so be sure that these are available in a nursing home before you decide to send your mother or father there.

28. Visit the Dining Hall

The dining hall is a place where residents can oftentimes fall through the cracks. Employees will not necessarily expect to see you in the dining hall, so you may be able to see their true colors as they deal with residents in the dining room. Look around the room and see if residents are sitting around for a long period of time, waiting for a staff member to bring them food. Also notice if residents that need help eating are assisted promptly, or if they have to sit and wait for long periods of time before a nurse or another staff member helps them. As residents are leaving the dining hall, try to get a quick glimpse of their appearance. Have their faces and clothes been cleaned of spilled food by a staff member? Or are the staff members too busy to pay attention to spilled food? These factors will help you understand how your parent will be treated should he or she become a resident of the nursing home.

29. Food

Along with the treatment of residents in the dining hall, while you are visiting, it is very important to take a look at the food itself. If you could taste the food, that would be ideal, but even if you can't, you can probably get a good sense of the food just by looking at it. Does it look and smell appetizing? Is it served on paper plates with plastic utensils, or is real silverware used? You should make sure that the food is appetizing and that it is served in an appetizing way.

Another important factor to consider when it comes to food is nutrition. You need to make sure that the food offered to your parent is going to be healthy and support a positive lifestyle. Take a look at what is being served in the cafeteria or dining hall. Are the plates full of colorful foods such as fruits and vegetables? Or are there a lot of cheap, heavy foods being served, like pasta, rice, and chicken?

Check out the menu for the week or even the month – it should be posted somewhere in the home. Make sure that the same three meals aren't repeated over the course of the month, that balanced meals are being prepared and served, and that residents can recommend their favorite meals. It is also important to make sure that there are alternatives to the meal being served that will cater to allergies, lifestyle choices such as vegetarianism, and any other dietary restrictions.

30. Visit at Different Times

Your visit to a nursing home can change drastically based on factors such as:

- Time of day
- Day of the week
- Nurses on duty
- Time of year

All of these factors and more will make a bad nursing home very different based on different visits. A good nursing home will remain consistent no matter what time it is, what day it is, or which staff members are on duty. After your initial visit to the nursing home, schedule another visit for a different time. Scheduling your second visit on a Friday or a Saturday night is a good idea. You can probably get into the dining room during dinner and see what kind of activities are planned for the evening. Nurses and other staff members on duty at this time may also be less patient with residents due to the fact that it is the weekend, so you will be able to see the staff's true colors at this time. Make sure that staff treatment remains the same or even improves during your second visit, but make sure that planned activities, meals, etc. are different. This will ensure that your parent gets consistent care, a good routine, and enough variety to keep life interesting.

31. Independence

One of the most important factors that will affect your parent's happiness in a nursing home is his or her independence. The nursing home is your parent's home. He or she should have the freedom to eat, wake up, exercise, socialize, go to sleep, etc. when he or she wants to. You should check to make sure that there are not severe restrictions on what your parent can do and when he or she can do it. Having the ability to make choices in his or her day-to-day life will help your parent feel confident and happy, and it will make the transition to living in a nursing home as smooth as possible.

32. Community

In the nursing home, there should be a sense of community

and even family among the members of the home. The residents should for the most part get along and enjoy each other's company, and the staff should be invested in making the nursing home as safe and happy as possible. The best nursing homes are the ones that view the home as a family. Staff and residents look out for one another and work well together towards a common goal. This sense of community can take a while to understand and cultivate, but when you visit, try to get a feel for the general environment of the home. If staff members love their jobs and residents are happy, you should be able to tell almost immediately.

COUNCIL MEETING INFORMATION

Residents are not the only people that you can talk to in order to gather information about the nursing home. Many nursing homes have councils for residents and their family members, so that they can have a say in actions taken against the nursing home. By attending one of these meetings and talking to members, you can learn about how residents and their family members impact change in the nursing home.

33. Attend a Council Meeting

In many nursing homes, the residents or the residents' family members will create a council to deal with issues that arise related to the home. These councils are usually referred to as resident councils or family councils, depending on the membership type and who runs the council. These types of councils are a good way to address any issues that arise in the nursing home and make further improvements by being proactive, brainstorming ideas, and establishing an organized way to approach the situation. If possible, you should attend one of the council meetings to see how they are run, what type of issues are addressed, and how these issues are resolved. If the nursing home that you are visiting doesn't have a resident or family council, there might not be an organized place for you to express your concerns, which might encourage you to consider other nursing homes that do have this option.

34. Council Membership

If you attend a resident or family council meeting, you should inquire about how you or your parent can become a member of the council. Being on the council will give your family influence over decisions made regarding the nursing home. Obtain information about membership eligibility and requirements for membership. If the family council will not allow you to be a member, this is not a good sign. If you want to be involved in the nursing home, be sure to find one who's family council will allow you to join.

35. Who Does the Council Report To?

When checking out the family or resident council, you should ask a member how decisions are reached and who the council reports to. For example, do all members get to vote on issues, or does one person or a board have the power to make decisions? Is there a hierarchy of power that the council must follow? Does the council have to report to a president or someone else in charge? Becoming a member of a family council is great, but if regular members don't have any say in how situations are handled, you need to be aware of this fact. You can either try to get on the council's board or seek a nursing home with a more democratic family council.

VISITING THE HOME: FORMAL INTERVIEW

When you schedule a visit with the nursing home, at least one staff member should be available to show you around or sit down and answer your questions. Many times, you will have the opportunity to meet with a nurse. If a nurse or the Director of Operations does not offer to speak with you, it is your responsibility to seek these people out. Speaking with these employees can help you understand the nursing home and if it is the right fit for your parent.

Speaking with a Nurse

When you visit a nursing home, talking to a nurse is one of the most important things that you can do. Below is a list of topics that you should be sure to cover with the nurse that you talk to. If you can talk to more than one staff member, for example, a head nurse, as well as a regular staff member, this is even better.

36. Types of Nurses

Not all nurses are created equal! There are different types of nurses, and it is important that you understand which types the nursing home employs, as well as their policies regarding these nurses. The main types of nurses that a nursing home might employ are:

- Registered Nurses
- Certified Nursing Assistants (CNAs)
- Licensed Vocational Nurses/Licensed Practical Nurses

A **registered nurse** is one who has passed a licensing exam, obtained a nursing license, and graduated from nursing school. A registered nurse should always oversee procedures concerning your parent in the nursing home. A registered nurse works with other types of nurses and assistants to establish care plans and treat residents in a nursing home. You should ask a staff member or a nurse who oversees treatment to make sure that it is a registered nurse that is in charge of your parent's care at all times.

A **certified nursing assistant** is a nurse's assistant and may provide basic care to residents in a nursing home, but only under the supervision of a member of the nursing staff. Basic care that a certified nursing assistant can provide includes feeding, dressing, grooming, and bathing residents, and other basic tasks. To become a certified nursing assistant, the assistant must undergo training and be licensed by the state. If you are speaking with a certified nursing assistant in the nursing home, ask him or her what kind of tasks he or she is in charge of and how much supervision he or she receives from the registered nurses in the facility. If a certified nursing assistant tells you that he or she does something like administer medication without the help of a registered nurse, this is a red flag. Certified nursing assistants should not have too much freedom in the nursing home because they are oftentimes not qualified to make medical decisions or handle residents on their own.

A **licensed vocational nurse** or **licensed practical nurse** are licensed nurses who can take care of sick, disabled, or injured residents. These nurses must be given direction from registered nurses, but are now supervised by physicians. Again, you should make sure that your parent's care is not entirely left to a licensed practical nurse, but rather, that a registered nurse is in charge of his or her treatment.

37. Staff Hours

It is very important that you do not pick a nursing home where the staff is overworked. Overworked and tired nurses are oftentimes burnt out, tired, and frustrated. This is a bad combination when working with residents that need compassionate and consistent care. When speaking with a staff member, you should subtly ask him or her what their hours are like. Before visiting the nursing home, you may be able to look up staff hours and shift rules on the nursing home's website, but if you cannot find this information, asking a nurse or another staff member can get you the answers that you need. Asking not only what a typical shift is like, but if shift rules are broken and how often will be telling. While staff members might not want to share this information, you might be able to speak honestly with a staff member about hours and shift schedules, which can help you make a decision about the nursing home.

38. Response Time

When you're considering a nursing home, you want to make sure that your parent will be a priority at the home that you choose. Every resident is important, and the nursing home should have the staff available to give each resident individualized and attentive care. One issue that I have seen in many nursing homes is nurses and other staff members making a resident wait for treatment. A staff member may have a slow response time for many different reasons. A few common reasons could be that he or she is socializing and not doing his or her job, there is poor communication among the staff about which residents need assistance, or the staff member is simply carrying too heavy of a workload, which makes residents slip through the cracks. It is important to talk to a staff member about his or her personal response time and the general response time of the staff to prevent these issues. Again, some staff members might not be very honest or accurate when it comes to these statistics, but this is an important question that is worth asking.

39. Staff to Resident Ratio

In order for your mother or father to receive the best care possible in a nursing home, he or she needs consistent and individualized attention. Most nursing homes have nurses that take care of specific residents during their shifts. It is important to make sure that the nurses and staff members do not have too many residents assigned to their care at one time. Think about it – if you are in charge of caring for 20 people, you will probably give each individual less attention and time than if you had 5 residents to look after. Ask nurses and other staff members roughly how many residents they are in charge of at any given time. This will give you a good idea of the staff to resident ratio. This ratio can greatly impact response time, treatment, and the likelihood of neglect and abuse.

40. Personal Licensing

If you can meet with the Director of Operations or another person in a leadership position, you can ask him or her about nurse and staff licensing policies in the nursing home. If you cannot meet with such personnel, it is important to talk to staff members about their credentials. Inquire about where they went to school, their licensing process, and if they are properly licensed for the job. Some nursing homes are not strict in making sure that their employees properly registered. This can lead to many medical and personal problems in a nursing home, so it is best to avoid a nursing home that has employed staff members who are not properly qualified.

41. Staff Turnover Rate

One of the biggest red flags when it comes to choosing a nursing home for your parent is the staff turnover rate. A high staff turnover rate indicates poor management, lack of communication between staff members, and the inability to make progress in a home. These factors oftentimes lead to neglect and abuse of residents. When you are speaking with a nurse or another staff member, ask him or her the following questions to develop an understanding of the staff turnover rate in the nursing home:

- How long have you been working here?
- Which staff member has been here the longest? How long has that person been here?
- Do you have any positions open for new staff members?
- Is it common for staff members to quit or get fired?

- How long do you plan on working here?

Questions such as these will help you determine the nature of the staff turnover rate and ultimately help you decide if this is a nursing home you want to consider or not.

42. Staff Interaction with Residents

Each nursing home is different. A nursing home may focus on hiring many registered nurses, or just a few registered nurses who oversee assistants and other staff members. Understanding what kind of staff members your parent will interact with as a resident will be essential in his or her care at this particular home. Asking staff members what kind of employees have the most interaction with residents can help you understand who your parent will be interacting with and these employees' qualifications. If you learn that most residents are primarily cared for by nursing assistants or other staff members with less training, you might want to consider another nursing home.

43. Preventative Care

You can see how attentive and committed to the health of its residents a nursing home is by learning about the home's preventative care policy. A good nursing home will take precautionary measures to nip health problems in the bud. Specialists should be regularly available to meet with residents and ensure that minor health issues do not evolve into large problems. Specialists such as dentists, eye doctors, foot doctors, ear doctors, etc. should be available to meet with residents. The nursing home that you choose should have a policy of listening to residents that complain about physical ailments and setting up appointments with a relevant specialist to get residents the treatment that they need. Check to see what forms, plans, or rules your home has in place.

44. Care Plan Creation

Care plans are the foundation of nursing home residents' health and well-being. A care plan should be created and carried out for every resident in the nursing home that you visit. Talk to a nurse about the care plans created for the residents in the nursing home and the process of creating a care plan for your loved one. You can ask the nurse questions such as:

- How do you typically create care plans for your residents?
- Can my family be part of the care plan process?
- If needed, can changes be made to the care plan? How are these changes made?
- Can I have a copy of the care plan?
- Which doctors will be included in the care plan?
- Who will carry out the care plan and make adjustments as necessary?

Creating the care plan is an essential step in your parent's health and well-being. Get a feel for what this process will be like before you commit to a nursing home.

45. Care Plan Implementation

Creating a care plan is great, but having a care plan means nothing if the plan won't be executed. You need to understand who will be in charge of executing the care plan and how often care plans are followed in the nursing home.

In general, it is always best to have a registered nurse execute a care plan or supervise others executing the care plan. This will make sure that nothing goes wrong from a medical standpoint. When talking with nurses and other staff members, you will be able to understand more about the execution of care plans by asking the following questions:

- Who is in charge of the care plans?
- Who makes sure that care plans are being followed?
- What happens if a care plan is violated?
- For the residents that you take care of, do you have their care plans on your person during the day?
- What do you do if a part of the care plan is not working well?
- Who is permitted to carry out care plans for residents?

Questions such as these will help you understand how care plans are implemented in the nursing home.

46. Medical Emergencies

It is not uncommon for medical emergencies to arise in a nursing home. You need to understand your nursing home's medical emergencies policy so that you will know how a sudden medical issue is dealt with. Talk to a nursing staff about their typical procedure when such an issue arises. Will a nurse try to figure out what is wrong first, or immediately call a doctor? When is a resident transported out of the nursing home? At what point in the process is the family contacted? Will the resident's home doctor be contacted? These are all worthwhile questions that will help you determine how well your parent will be cared for in the event of a medical emergency.

SPEAKING WITH THE DIRECTOR OF OPERATIONS

If possible, you should try to get in touch with the Director of Operations or another person who is in charge of overseeing the nursing home. Speaking with such a supervisor can help you understand many of the procedures that the nursing home abides by. In addition, you will be able to get answers to questions that staff members themselves may hesitate to answer. Keep the following tips in mind when talking to a Director of Operations.

47. Visiting Policy

Chances are, you will want to visit your loved one regularly while he or she is living in a nursing home. You can discuss the visiting policy with the Director of Operations. Many nursing homes will work with the family to find the best times for visiting. On special occasions such as birthdays and anniversaries, some nursing homes will set up a private room for you and your family to have a party. Even if the nursing home does not offer this option, you should make sure that it has regular, ample visiting hours. Visiting on nights and weekends is possible in good nursing homes, so be sure to ask about this opportunity as well as visiting on or near holidays.

48. Contacting Loved Ones

It is important to make sure that your parent has access to a phone or a computer so as to communicate with family and friends at his or her discretion. Your parent should not have restrictions on when they can contact friends and family members, unless a special circumstance arises. Be sure to ask about the policy for contacting people outside of the home.

49. Emergency Evacuation Plan

There should be many plans in place in order to protect your parent and all other nursing home residents. One such plan is an emergency evacuation plan. Ask about what happens if all residents have to be escorted out of the building due to a fire or another dangerous event. Does the nursing home have clearly labeled exits and emergency exits? Does the nursing home run fire alarm drills periodically to help staff members and residents understand what to do if they need to evacuate the facility for any reason? Having a comprehensive emergency evacuation plan in place and making sure that both residents and staff members know how to execute this plan is essential for the safety of your parent.

50. Abuse Prevention Policy

One of the best ways to prevent neglect and abuse is for a nursing home to have a comprehensive abuse prevention policy that all residents and staff members are familiar with. Ask the Director of Operations if the nursing home has such a policy and review the policy with your parent. Knowing that there are safeguards in place to protect your parent and all residents from neglect and abuse can help you feel at ease. By clearly outlining what is and is not allowed in the nursing home, as well as establishing penalties for neglect and abuse, the amount of neglect and abuse incidents can be greatly diminished. Ask about training on this issue, and if this is documented in the records of the home.

51. Complaint Policy

If you and your parent are considering a nursing home that you are visiting, you need to be aware of how the nursing home deals with conflict. Even the best nursing homes have issues, and if you have a problem with the nursing home, you need to know whom you can contact about your concerns and what will be done about them. Ask the Director of Operations where you can make a complaint and how complaints are handled. Will someone get back to you in a timely manner? Will efforts be made to find a solution to the problem at hand? Will the nursing home follow up with you to make sure that you are satisfied with the way that the issue was handled? You need the answers to these questions so that you can be confident that if any issues arise, you and your parent's needs will be addressed.

52. Examples of Conflict Resolution

Having a complaint policy in place is great, but if the policy isn't followed, it won't do much good. A nursing home employee might assure you that your complaints and recommendations will be given the respect that they deserve, but in practice, this might not be the case. Ask the Director of Operations about specific instances where staff members, residents, and residents' family members have made recommendations or complaints that were listened to. Ask about the procedure for dealing with these issues and if change was actually implemented. If the Director can quickly and easily provide you with a few specific examples, you can be confident that the nursing home is dedicated to improvement.

53. Complaint History

If possible, you should talk to the Director of Operations about viewing previous complaints made against the nursing home. You can also view complaints of neglect and abuse made to the police department by contacting the police department itself. An extensive complaint history will not reflect well on the nursing home.

54. Future Improvement Plans

Part of a clear dedication to improving a nursing home is it's future plans for development. Talk to the Director of Operations about the nursing home's plans to improve in the future. Some common examples of improvements to look out for are:

- Purchasing newer models of equipment
- Paying for nurses and other employees to continue their training
- Adding a new wing to the facility
- Implementing a staff screening process, abuse prevention policy, care plan policy, etc. if the nursing home does not have these things already

- Restructuring management
- Providing additional in-house treatment
- Making rooms more comfortable for residents
- Adding new activities for the residents
- Improving meal plans
- Monitoring staff more carefully
- Hiring more registered nurses
- Extending visiting hours

There are always ways to enhance a facility. The Director of Operations should recognize this and have plans to make the nursing home even better.

55. Screening Process for Staff Members

All potential employees should be thoroughly vetted before they are offered positions at a nursing home. Not only should it be clear that they have completed the schooling, training, and licensing necessary to hold a position as a nurse or another staff member of a nursing home, but nursing homes should also check to make sure that their employees do not have a history of violence or behavioral issues. Nurses and other staff members who have been arrested for assault or other violent crimes are at a greater risk for causing neglect and abuse. These candidates should not be accepted as employees of a nursing home, or, if they are given a position, they should be carefully monitored and evaluated frequently. If you ask a Director of Operations about what the nursing home looks for in potential employees, and the director does not mention a screening process, this should raise some concern. For the safety of your parent, it is important to make sure that he or she is treated by compassionate, caring people – not those with a violent streak. You should also make sure that it is not just nurses who are screened, but all potential employees. Abuse can be committed by anyone in a nursing home – from the head nurse to a janitor.

56. Staff Training

Before beginning their jobs, all staff members should undergo a training process. Even experienced nurses will not know how this specific nursing home works upon arrival, so it is important that each staff member is properly and carefully trained. This will improve communication among staff members and ensure that each new employee is capable of working in the nursing home. Be sure to ask the Director of Operations about the training process for new employees. The more thorough this process is, the better.

57. Continued Education

It is not enough to just make sure that staff members have the proper qualifications and training to work in a nursing home. Laws, rules, and health practices are constantly changing, and it is important that all employees of a nursing home are kept up-to-date on these changes. Be sure to ask the Director of Operations what kind of continued staff training the employees receive. Again, it is important that it isn't just the nurses who receive continued training, but that all employees get this training. If there is proof that every staff member must fulfill a certain number of hours each year to continued training, this is a good sign.

58. Spiritual Services

The nursing home that you are visiting should meet the spiritual and religious needs of your parent as well as all other residents. Religious needs are fairly straightforward. They oftentimes include:

- Access to religious services
- Access to a religious leader for guidance
- Last rites
- Bible study or a way to share faith with others
- Accommodations for certain dietary restrictions
- Access to religious texts
- Religious sacraments (such as baptism, confession, etc.)

Most nursing homes do not hesitate to provide these services. However, spiritual needs can be more difficult to define and meet. Spirituality is any action that provides healing or meaning in one's life. People can find spirituality in exercise, music, art, the company of their loved ones, meditation, etc. A nursing home should allow residents the freedom to explore their own spirituality and the resources to experience it. If your parent is religious or spiritual, be sure to ask about specific ways that the nursing home meets these needs.

59. Social Services

All nursing homes should have social services available to their residents. This is meant to provide quality care for residents as well as an outlet in the event that the residents need help or feel that they have been neglected or abused. Some common examples of social services include:

- Counseling
- Improved care
- Improved living conditions
- Someone to talk to in the event of neglect or abuse

If your parent ever feels uncomfortable in the nursing home, if he or she has a difficult time transitioning, or if he or she has been neglected or abused, he or she should contact social services. Make sure that social services are available to all residents before you decide on a nursing home.

60. In House Treatment

If your parent has medical issues that require constant care, you should make sure that the nursing home you are visiting has the capacity to deal with these issues. It will be much easier, cheaper, and less stressful for your parent if he or she can receive treatment at the nursing home instead of having to constantly be transported to a hospital or a doctor's office to get treatment. If your parent can be treated in house, you will also be aware of who is treating your parent and you will have the opportunity to easily communicate with him or her through the nursing home.

The more forms of treatment that the nursing home offers, the better. Be sure to talk to the nursing staff about what kind of treatments they are qualified to perform. You can also talk to the Director of Operations about the type of equipment that the nursing home has.

61. Contracts

If you think that you've found the right nursing home, and

you're ready to move your parent into the home, many facilities will ask you to sign a contract first. Before you sign anything, you need to protect your parent by having a lawyer carefully look over the documents. Some nursing homes put an arbitration clause in the fine print of their contracts. An arbitration clause states that any issues must be solved through an arbitration process. This means that if your parent is neglected or abused in the home, you may not be able to file a lawsuit against the nursing home. Having a lawyer look over the contract can alert you to an arbitration clause or anything that seems out of the ordinary in the document.

INFORMATION TO GIVE THE NURSING HOME

When you have decided on a nursing home, you can prevent miscommunication, neglect, and abuse by providing the home with detailed information about your parent and your family. If your parent is already in a nursing home, and you realize that the home does not have some of this information, it is never too late to provide it.

62. Medical History

There is some information that you can provide a nursing home with to ensure that medical errors, neglect, and abuse do not occur. One such way to reduce the risk of these issues is by providing the nursing home with a detailed list of your parent's medical history. Be sure to make the nursing staff aware of information such as:

- Family medical history
- Basic information such as sex/date of birth/ethnicity, etc.
- Blood type
- History of surgeries that your parent has had
- History of any diseases or illnesses that your parent has had

- History of vaccinations and medications that your parent has received
- Any mental health conditions
- Current medical conditions
- Lifestyle habits, for example, information about smoking, drug use, alcohol use, diet, exercise routines, etc.
- Allergies

Providing the nursing home with detailed information regarding your parent's medical history will help prepare the staff to treat your parent. Many issues that arise can be easily fixed with proper knowledge of a resident's medical history. Having this information can also prevent certain medical errors.

63. Special Needs Information

Another type of information that you should provide to the nursing home is any information regarding your parent's special needs. In some cases, a nursing home may not have the resources to properly treat your parent, given his or her special circumstances. It is best to provide this information as soon as possible so that you can learn about the nursing home's resources and create a care plan that will accommodate your parent. If you do not feel that the nursing home can or will give special attention to your parent's needs, it is best to find another nursing home. Creating the right care plan for your parent's needs or eliminating a home from your search that won't cater to your parent's needs can prevent neglect, abuse, and medical errors down the road.

64. Insurance Information

Getting the logistics taken care of as soon as possible is always a plus when picking a nursing home. Talk to the Director of Operations or another employee about what kind of insurance the nursing home accepts and how you can go about making payments. Some common forms of insurance that a nursing home will accept include:

- Medicare
- Medicaid
- Private insurance
- Veterans administration aid
- Long-term care insurance
- Health insurance

Communicating with the nursing home about how the bills will be paid for is an essential step in making sure that your parent is comfortable in the home.

65. Current Health Status Information

The current health of your parent is just as important as your parent's medical history. You need to inform the nursing home of any current diseases, illnesses, injuries, surgeries, etc. that your parent has experienced. Providing an up-to-date list of current medication is also essential in making sure that your parent gets the right treatment in the nursing home. You should be as specific as possible when providing all of this information – particularly information regarding medication. This will help nurses and nursing staff when administering medication and it can prevent medical errors. Clearly providing this information will combat an employee's statement that he or she didn't know about your parent's medical conditions in the event that an issue occurs. This information should be updated periodically as the status of your parent's health changes.

66. List of Health Care Providers

While your parent will receive treatment from nurses, doctors, and other nursing home staff members, it is a good idea to provide the nursing home with information about your parent's past or current health care providers. A clear list of contact information for your parent's doctors will give the nursing home communication options if they have questions regarding your parent's health or medical history. Providing this information from the beginning will make the process of obtaining vital information regarding your parent's health as simple and easy as it can be for the nursing home. If your parent is already in a nursing home, and the home does not yet have this information, it is never too late to provide it. As with the other information that you should provide, you can give this information to the nursing home at any time. Be sure to keep a copy for yourself!

67. Emergency Contacts

You and your family should designate one person who will primarily communicate with the nursing home. This person should be in charge of contacting the nursing home in the event of an issue, if a complaint has to be made, or if you simply need information regarding your parent. While this person will primarily deal with the nursing home, it is a good idea to provide the home with a comprehensive list of emergency contacts for your parent. Within this list of contacts, you can provide information for relevant parties, such as your parent's:

- Family members
- Lawyer
- Doctor(s)
- Colleagues

Having this information readily available will ensure that you and other people are contacted in a timely manner if there is ever an issue.

68. Create a Will

In order to protect your parent's assets and prepare for the future, it is a good idea to establish a Will before your parent goes into a nursing home or while he or she is in a nursing home. This will ensure that your parent has funeral plans and other preparations created. It will also ensure that your parent's assets are protected and that potential beneficiaries' interests are protected. A Will can also protect your parent's health care needs.

Another way to protect your parent is by invoking a power of attorney or having an attorney review paperwork and policies related to the nursing home. If there is anything that leaves your parent vulnerable to neglect or abuse in the structure of the nursing home or in the paperwork, a lawyer will be able to catch it and advise you on how to proceed. These precautionary measures will outline and protect your parent's health care needs, assets, and more.

69. Create an Account for Personal Needs

To protect both your parent's personal interests and his or her health, you should consider opening a personal needs account that the nursing home can manage. You and your family can deposit money into this account, and the nursing home and your parent can manage the account to ensure that your parent's needs are met. Instead of giving the nursing home access to all of your parent's finances, this is a good way to ensure that your parent is not taken advantage of, but that he or she still has access to money for personal use.

IDENTIFYING ABUSE

Increased Risk Factors

When analyzing nursing home residents that are neglected and abused, research has shown that there are several risk factors that can increase a resident's likelihood of being neglected or abused. Of course, this does not mean that just because your parent exhibits one of these risk factors that he or she will definitely be neglected or abused. However, it is important to understand these risks so that you can help your parent as much as possible.

70. Dementia

While all elderly people could be the victim of neglect or abuse, there are a few factors that can increase an elderly person's risk for neglect or abuse. One of these risk factors is memory loss. Whether your parent has been diagnosed with dementia, Alzheimer's disease, or another form of memory loss, you should be particularly alert to his or her treatment in a nursing home.

Some perpetrators of abuse see those with dementia as easy targets. This is because the victim is likely to forget the abuse – whether it is physical, sexual, financial, or some other form of abuse. A nursing home employee might target those with memory issues because the likelihood of the victim reporting the abuse is lower in these situations. If this is the case, it is important that you stay vigilant and check for warning signs of abuse each time you visit your parent. Many warning signs of neglect, physical abuse, and sexual abuse will be visible, although other types of abuse such as emotional abuse will be harder to identify. Still, it is important to make sure that you are comfortable with the nursing home that you have chosen and that you are present in your parent's life so that you can prevent or recognize any form of abuse.

71. Disability

Another factor that can increase the risk for neglect or abuse for a nursing home resident is having a disability. There are several reasons for this fact. One reason for this is that a physical or mental disability will make the resident more reliant on the assistance of the nursing staff. This can cause issues such as rough handling, verbal abuse, force-feeding, bedsores, and neglect based on the resident's specific needs. Another reason that a disability can increase the risk for neglect and abuse is that a staff member of a nursing home may be aware that the resident will be unable to defend him or herself.

Of course, a resident with a disability will not automatically be neglected or abused, however, you need to understand that your parent's risk of neglect or abuse will increase if he or she has a disability.

72. Gender

It is more common for female nursing home residents to be neglected or abused than male nursing home residents. Again, this does not mean that men will not be abused in a nursing home, but women tend to be victims of certain types of abuse, such as sexual and physical abuse, more often than men are. One reason for this statistic is that women are oftentimes physically more vulnerable than men. This means that if your mother is going to live in a nursing home, you should be on the lookout for signs of neglect or abuse.

73. Financial Situation

When it comes to types of abuse such as physical or sexual abuse, a nursing home resident's financial situation probably will not be a major factor in the abuse; however, for other types of abuse, such as insurance fraud, healthcare fraud, or financial abuse, this can play a large role. It may seem obvious to you that those in good financial standings will be targeted for financial abuse more often than residents that do not have a lot to offer financially. If your parent is wealthy, or even just appears to be wealthy due to his or her expensive possessions, you should make sure that he or she is protected from fraud or any type of financial abuse. Be sure to keep valuables in a nursing home out of view. If possible, you should make sure that they are locked away. Refraining from talking about your parent's financial situation with the nursing staff can also protect your parent from financial abuse.

74. Emotional and Mental State

Your parent's emotional stability can be a factor in abuse in a nursing home. Sometimes, nursing home employees target those who are different when it comes to neglect and abuse. The staff may force your parent to become more unstable by withholding medication for depression or other mental illnesses, or provoking your parent with emotional and physical abuse. Neglect and abuse for someone who is already dealing with mental instability will only make this worse. Be sure to monitor your parent's emotional health consistently as he or she transitions into life in the nursing home. Checking in to make sure that the care plan includes your parent's medication and that this medication is being provided will be important in keeping your parent happy and healthy. If your parent is suffering from a mental illness, by understanding that this is a risk factor for abuse, you can protect your parent.

75. Social Life

Loneliness can actually be a factor in neglect and abuse because those who are having a difficult time transitioning to nursing home life can become targets for different types of abuse. Your parent might be too trusting of the staff members due to his or her desire to make friends, which could lead to financial abuse. To prevent this situation, make sure that you encourage your parent to make friends with other residents. Having a social network within the nursing home will also ensure that people notice if your parent is acting strangely or if there are clear signs of abuse. This awareness can assist your parent in getting the help that he or she needs. When you call your parent, ask if he or she is making friends and developing a strong social life within the nursing home. To prevent loneliness, you can also visit the nursing home and call your parent on a regular basis.

76. Education Level

Some studies indicate that education level can play a part in the neglect and abuse of the elderly. Those with lower education levels, for example, residents who did not finish high school or did not go to college, tend to be victims of neglect and abuse more than residents with advanced degrees. Those who commit neglect and abuse tend to steer clear of those who may be well connected or those who will know how to handle neglect and abuse, such as former doctors, lawyers, professors, etc.

COMMON TYPES OF ABUSE

77. Bedsores

There are many different types of injuries that a loved one may get in a nursing home. In this section, I will discuss some of the most common injuries and medical issues that may arise in a nursing home.

One of the most common forms of injury that a person can sustain in a nursing home is a bedsore, also known as a pressure sore. A bedsore is an injury to skin and tissue underneath skin caused by extensive pressure on a part of the body. Bedsores generally develop when a person does not move for long periods of time. If nursing home employees neglect residents, bedsores are a common development. Bedsores commonly develop in areas such as:

- Ankles
- Heels
- Tailbone.
- Spine
- Shoulder blades
- Elbows
- Hips

These body parts are common areas where bedsores develop because there isn't a lot of fat or muscle to protect the bone from pressure.

When blood flow to tissue and skin is limited due to prolonged pressure with no relief (movement), tissue and skin cells will become damaged and can eventually die. Friction can aggravate or worsen a bedsore. This may occur when your parent tries to move or a care provider attempts to move your parent. Another factor in nursing homes that contribute to bedsores is called shear. Shear is when two forces are moving in opposite directions. For example, in a hospital bed that is elevated, your parent might begin slipping toward the bottom of the bed. Your parent's skin will start pulling in a downward direction, but the bones will stay put. This force can create a bedsore.

Bedsores are extremely common in nursing homes due to the inattention of nurses and other staff members. If residents are not consistently and carefully moved, stretched out, and allowed to walk, bedsores will develop. If you suspect that your parent has a bedsore, look for common symptoms such as ulcers, scabs, redness, swelling, pain, bleeding, etc. If you find bedsores, you may want to contact a lawyer.

78. Malnutrition

Neglect of nursing home residents will oftentimes lead to malnutrition or malnourishment. Sometimes, employees will withhold meals from residents if they are angry with them or to see them suffer. Other times, employees will only provide limited and non-nutritional food to residents, causing malnourishment.

Common symptoms of these issues include:

- Weight loss
- Brittle bones
- Dizziness

- Dehydration
- Fatigue

If malnutrition or malnourishment go untreated, they can cause mental or physical disability. As soon as you begin noticing these symptoms, it is important to address them by getting in touch with a doctor. While these symptoms may be caused by an underlying condition or disease, malnourishment and malnutrition can also indicate neglect or abuse. Keep an eye on your loved one if you suspect an employee has caused malnutrition in your parent and don't be afraid to get help.

79. Falls

For elderly people, falls can be very common and also very dangerous. For many families, recognizing that mom or dad is falling down frequently is a sign that he or she needs additional care and can no longer live alone. Nursing homes are supposed to reduce the number of dangerous falls that your parent has. While sometimes accidents do happen, falls in nursing homes should be prevented by proper assistance from staff members.

Falls can lead to very serious problems for elderly people. Falls in the elderly are commonly caused by:

- Loss of balance
- Improper medication type or level
- Muscle weakness
- Slow reflexes
- Confusion
- Changes in blood pressure
- Vision issues
- Cardiovascular disorder

- Infection
- Need for change of treatment for a particular condition

Falling down can also cause serious problems for elderly people, including:

- Bruising
- Cuts
- Broken bones - some that need surgery to repair
- Head injuries
- Spinal injuries

In a nursing home, the hope is that falls can be prevented due to the attentive care and assistance of qualified staff members looking out for your parent. If a fall occurs anyway, a staff member may be neglecting his or her duties or purposefully failing to help your parent. While not all falls are a result of foul play, some falls can be. Make sure to carefully investigate the fall if one occurs. If a fall has occurred and your loved one is injured, you should consult with an attorney.

80. Medical Errors

A medical error is a negative effect of care by a doctor, nurse, or other care provider. In order to be defined as a medical error, the issue must have been preventable, and it must be caused by the negligence, recklessness, or carelessness of the provider. A few common examples of medical errors include an incomplete or inaccurate treatment or diagnosis of:

- Injury
- Disease
- Syndrome
- Infection

- Behavior

Just as with falls in nursing homes, not all medical errors are purposeful. Lack of communication, lack of knowledge, poor focus, and other factors can cause a care provider to commit a medical error. However, in some cases, a care provider will purposefully misdiagnose or mistreat an issue in order to inflict pain on a resident. If this is the case, the resident has been abused, and getting him or her out of this situation is in your best interest. If you suspect that your parent has been misdiagnosed or treated improperly, you should seek help immediately from a lawyer.

81. Medication Errors

A very common example of abuse in nursing homes is a medication error. A medication error is defined as any event that leads someone to administer an inappropriate type or amount of medication to a patient. For the event to be defined as a medication error, it must have been preventable by proper treatment. Sometimes, medication errors are not committed on purpose. A nurse may misread a prescription label or forget to give a resident his or her medication, but did not purposefully cause harm to the resident. In this case, a medication error would still occur, but the nurse or other staff member could argue that the medication error was an accident. In other cases, nurses may deprive residents of pain medication, administer the wrong dosage, or cause another type of medication error on purpose. To determine the nature of a medication error, you should talk openly and honestly with your parent. A medication error could be negligence and that could be the basis of a lawsuit.

PREVENTING AND RECOGNIZING ABUSE

82. Continued Communication with Staff

Once your parent is settled in a nursing home, the communication between you and the home should not stop. Even the best nursing homes make mistakes, and even the best employees get confused. Issues may come up, but you don't want your parent to suffer as a result of them. To prevent as many issues as possible, and to make sure that your parent is not a victim of neglect or abuse, you need to keep in constant communication with the nursing home staff. Checking in with the staff once a week or once a month will ensure that everything is running smoothly. If you have questions or the staff has questions, these can be addressed during regular communication. Whether you send an email or stop by the nurses' station while visiting your parent, checking in for a few minutes can make a world of difference in your parent's treatment. You can prevent honest mistakes and show the staff that you are involved in your parent's life. Any neglect or abuse will not go unnoticed because you are constantly there, making sure that your parent is happy and healthy. This is the value of being a consistent presence in the nursing home and in the staff's lives.

83. Continued Communication with Your Parent

Many times, neglect and abuse go unreported, because victims are hesitant to discuss the situation with other people. They may feel in some way responsible for what happened to them, embarrassed about the situation, or fearful that telling someone will only make the situation worse. If your parent is being mistreated or neglected, you do not want him or her to feel this way. Regular communication with your parent will help you get a sense of his or her schedule and if anything seems out of the ordinary in the nursing home. By consistently visiting and calling your parent, you will show him or her that you are involved in his or her life and you will not tolerate neglect or abuse by the nursing home. Even if your parent does not feel comfortable discussing neglect and abuse, by visiting consistently, you can recognize the warning signs of abuse and confront your parent about it if you suspect that neglect or abuse has taken place.

Even if you have properly investigated a nursing home and feel confident in putting your parent in the home, your work is not done once he or she moves in. You should keep an eye on your parent in the event that any issues arise. The following tips are meant to help you identify all of the different types of neglect and abuse that your parent may experience in a nursing home. If you begin to notice any of these signs, or if your parent tells you that he or she has been neglected and abused, you need to begin taking action. Documenting the abuse, getting your parent out of the nursing home, and reporting the abuse are good places to start.

84. Common Examples of Physical Abuse

Physical abuse is defined as any unwanted and intentional physical contact. This is a common form of abuse in many nursing homes. Common examples of physical abuse in nursing homes include, but are not limited to:

- Beating
- Bleeding
- Broken bones
- Bruises
- Burns
- Cuts
- Difficulty walking or sitting
- Force feeding
- Imprint injuries
- Sprains
- Use of physical restraints

Watch out for these injuries. If you notice any of them, inquire about them when talking to your parent.

85. Warning Signs of Physical Abuse

If you noticed one of the injuries mentioned above, and you suspect that it was the result of physical abuse, you should keep your eye out for common warning signs of physical abuse. These include:

- Any unexplained changes in behavior
- Confession of abuse
- Dehydration
- Depression
- Difficulty sleeping

- Fear of being touched
- Fear of going to the bathroom or bathing
- Fear of a person or a place
- Improper hygiene
- Poor grooming
- Regression to childlike behavior
- Skin breakdown
- Sudden nightmares
- Visible injuries
- Weight loss

If you notice any of these changes in your loved one, you should seek help immediately to determine the cause and fix the problem.

86. Common Examples of Sexual Abuse

Sexual abuse is any unwanted and intentional sexual contact. Residents with dementia or female residents have a higher chance of being victims of sexual abuse than other residents. Some common examples of sexual abuse include:

- All types of sexual battery
- Coerced nudity
- Rape
- Sexually explicit photography
- Sodomy
- Unwanted touching

These sexual offenses and others should not be tolerated in any nursing home. If you suspect such an act, you should seek help for your parent immediately.

87. Warning Signs of Sexual Abuse

Sexual abuse is an issue that should be taken care of as soon as possible. If you suspect that your parent has been a victim of sexual abuse, look for the following signs to confirm your suspicions:

- Any sudden changes in behavior
- Anxiety
- Bleeding in genitals, anus, or mouth
- Changes in eating habits
- Discharges in genitals, anus, or mouth
- Discoloration in genitals, anus, or mouth
- Pain in genitals, anus, or mouth
- Pain in urination/bowel movements
- Promiscuity
- Resisted removal of clothing at appropriate times
- Self-injury
- Sudden wetting and soiling accidents
- Torn, stained, or bloody undergarments
- Venereal disease

Some of these signs might have nothing to do with abuse, but if you notice any of them, you should keep a close eye on your parent.

88. Common Examples of Emotional and Psychological Abuse

Emotional and psychological abuse are constituted by any intentional act that is meant to reduce a person's self-esteem and self-worth. It can be more difficult to define and prove emotional abuse than physical abuse because there will not be any physical proof of them. Instead, you have to go off of how the victim felt and the emotional damage that was done. A few common examples of this type of abuse include:

- Enforced social isolation
- Harassment
- Humiliation
- Insults
- Intimidation
- Isolation from family, friends, or regular activities
- Silent treatment
- Treating the resident like an infant
- Threats
- Verbal assaults

While emotional abuse is harder to prove than other types of abuse, it is a serious crime. If you have noticed any of the above examples when visiting your parent in a nursing home, you need to get help immediately.

89. Warning Signs of Emotional or Psychological Abuse

If you've noticed examples of emotional abuse in the nursing home that your parent is a resident of, you should start paying attention to warning signs to confirm the abuse. A few common warning signs of this type of abuse are:

- Behavioral changes
- Depression
- Emotional outbursts
- Fear of a particular person or place
- Mood swings
- Sudden anger

For residents that are having a difficult time adjusting to nursing home life, these actions might be normal. However, these can also be signs of emotional abuse. Be sure to stay involved in your parent's life to determine if abuse is occurring in the nursing home.

90. Common Examples of Neglect

Neglect occurs when the nursing home staff fails to provide basic needs for a resident. The motivation behind neglect can vary. In some cases, staff members may forget that they are supposed to take care of a particular resident, or there is poor communication between the staff regarding who needs to take care of which resident. In other cases, neglect can be done deliberately to harm a resident. A few common examples of neglect include deprivation of appropriate:

- Clothing
- Comfort
- Food
- Hygiene
- Medicine
- Personal safety
- Shelter
- Temperature in the building or room
- Water

Regardless of the reason for motivation, it should never be inflicted on your parent. If you learn that your parent has been neglected in a nursing home, you need to get him or her help as soon as possible.

91. Warning Signs of Neglect

If you suspect that your loved one has been the victim of neglect in a nursing home, look out for these warning signs to confirm your concerns:

- Bedsores
- Being left dirty or failure to bathe your parent
- Dehydration
- Desertion in a public place
- Malnutrition
- Unsafe living conditions
- Unsanitary living conditions
- Untreated physical problems
- Unusual weight loss

These warning signs might confirm that the neglect of your parent has taken place.

92. Common Examples of Financial Abuse

Financial abuse can occur if someone takes advantage of another person's financial situation. The elderly are oftentimes targets of financial abuse due to many factors. Because many elderly people need someone to assist them, such as a nurse, they become dependent on the help of others. This dependency on a stranger coupled with the fact that some elderly people don't have family members checking in on them can lead a caregiver to take advantage of the elderly person financially. Of course this is not always the case, but elderly people are at a higher risk for financial abuse than other people are. A few common examples of financial abuse include:

- Cashing checks without the permission of the elderly person
- Coercion into signing a document
- Deceit to sign a document
- Forged signatures
- Investment fraud
- Misuse of money or possessions
- Stealing of money or possessions
- Stolen identity

93. Warning Signs of Financial Abuse

To determine financial abuse, you need to keep a close eye on your parent's accounts and financial situation. Watch out for:

- Addition of a name to a signature card
- Changes to a Will, title, policy, or power of attorney
- Changes in financial condition
- Large withdrawals from accounts
- Missing cash or possessions
- Phony account activity
- Scams
- Unnecessary subscriptions to goods or services
- Unpaid bills

If you notice any suspicious activity related to your parent's financial accounts, your parent may be the victim of financial abuse.

94. Common Examples of Healthcare Fraud

Healthcare fraud occurs when someone files dishonest or false health care claims so that they can profit from these claims. Elderly people are oftentimes the victims of healthcare fraud because they are vulnerable and may need to rely on the assistance of others. This can be taken advantage of and healthcare fraud can ensue. Some common examples of this type of fraud are:

- Charging for healthcare without providing the healthcare services
- Double billing for medical care
- Kickbacks for referrals or drug prescriptions
- Medicaid or Medicare fraud
- Over or under medicating your parent
- Overcharging for medical care
- Recommending fraudulent solutions to medical conditions

Be sure to watch out for issues such as the ones mentioned above when your parent is in a nursing home.

95. Warning Signs of Healthcare Fraud

If you think that a nursing home employee is guilty of healthcare fraud, watch for these warning signs:

- A sales representative asks for your parent's financial information before a policy is even issued
- You can't get hard facts and information about a healthcare option or deal
- Your parent has received many phone calls or emails related to deals that seem too good to be true
- Your parent's medical bills aren't being paid
- Your parent never receives an insurance card

If you run into these issues, healthcare fraud may have taken place. Be sure to keep copies of any documentation that can support a healthcare fraud claim.

96. Common Examples of Insurance Fraud

Insurance fraud is defined by an action that intends to defraud a person or a company through some form of the insurance process. There are many different forms of insurance fraud, but some of the most common ones include:

- Abandoned house fraud
- Car damage fraud
- Health insurance fraud
- Renter's insurance fraud
- Unnecessary medical procedures

While elderly people are not always targets for all of the forms of insurance fraud mentioned above, you should still be aware of them. In some cases, insurance fraud may occur at the same time as other forms of financial fraud. Watch out for these issues on behalf of your parent.

97. Warning Signs of Insurance Fraud

If your parent experiences any of these issues, he or she may be a victim of insurance fraud:

- False information related to a company
- False records
- Illegal kickbacks
- Lack of a bill of service
- Low premiums

- Pressure to sign a document
- Suspicious billing

Protect your loved one from insurance fraud by looking out for these issues.

98. Common Examples of Medical Errors

A medical error is the negligence of health care that could have been prevented. For example, any inaccurate treatment or diagnosis could be considered a medical error. While medical errors are oftentimes committed accidentally, this does not mean that the person that committed the error is not responsible. His or her negligence or recklessness contributed to the error, and he or she can be financially and legally responsible for the offense. A few common medical errors are:

- Bedsores
- Errors in the lab
- Infection from surgery
- Injuries from falls
- Issues with medication
- Misdiagnosis
- Treatment errors
- Urinary tract infections from catheter issues

99. Warning Signs of Medical Errors

If you suspect that your parent has been the victim of a medical error, you should look for the following warning signs:

- Admittance of misdiagnosis
- Admittance of mistreatment

- Any adverse effect of treatment or diagnosis
- Breach of duty of care
- Infection
- Negligence
- Poor communication among staff members
- Poor resident and staff communication
- Sudden change in diagnosis
- Sudden change in treatment

100. Common Examples of Discrimination

Discrimination is defined as unfair treatment of a person based on a category that he or she falls into. For example, people can be discriminated against based on their race, gender, gender identity, disability, age, etc. Residents in nursing homes should be free from all types of discrimination. A few common examples of discrimination are:

- Harassment
- Refusing to accept someone as a resident due to race, gender, religion, etc.
- Unfair treatment/special treatment for others
- Receiving the worst room in the home based on gender, race, religion, etc.
- Having to wait for treatment, food, etc. based on gender, disability, race, etc.
- Exclusion from certain activities

101. Warning Signs of Discrimination

Discrimination can happen to anyone for a multitude of reasons. A few common warning signs of discrimination that you should look for include:

- Noticing that some staff members are prejudiced against certain groups
- Special treatment for some residents
- Noticing that your parent does not have access to the resources that other residents have
- Abuse
- Neglect
- Depression or insecurity in your parent

If you notice any of these warning signs, your parent may be a victim of discrimination. Be sure to discuss this situation with your parent and with the nursing home staff.

BONUS CONTENT: 10 STEPS TO TAKE AFTER YOU SUSPECT ABUSE

We've given you over one hundred different ways to identify and prevent nursing home neglect and abuse. But what happens once you realize that your parent has been abused as a resident of a home? You need to know what actions to take in order to get your parent help and rectify this situation. Here are 10 steps that you can take after you suspect abuse to get your parent the help that he or she needs.

1. Talk to Your Parent

Admitting abuse can be extremely difficult for your parent. In some cases, he or she might inform you of the abuse as soon as it takes place, but in other cases, your parent might keep quiet about the abuse, and it's up to you to notice it and discuss it with your parent. Before you file a complaint or take other actions, you should confirm with your parent that abuse has taken place. Go somewhere private to talk and discuss the warning signs that you have noticed with your parent. Remember to be gentle, as discussing this issue is probably very difficult for your parent. Be sure to make it clear that your parent is not to blame if he or she is a victim of any kind of abuse. Your parent might not even be aware that what he or she has experienced is considered abuse, especially in the case of neglect, emotional abuse, or financial abuse, as these are not always clear-cut forms of abuse. Ask your parent if he or she has been abused, discriminated against, or taken advantage of in any way.

If you can confirm the abuse, you can move forward with getting your parent help. Be sure to listen to what your parent is saying and how he or she feels about the situation. In this situation, you should respect your parent's wishes while protecting him or her. Different people wish to deal with abuse in different ways, so be sure to truly listen to what your parent wants and read between the lines. Clear communication will allow you to understand how you should move forward in this situation.

2. File a Written Complaint with the Nursing Home

Each nursing home will have different procedures for dealing with a complaint of neglect or abuse. You should notify the nursing home of the abuse as soon as it is confirmed to begin the necessary processes. Notifying the nursing home as soon as possible will make the process that the nursing home has to go through as quick as possible, which will bring you and your family one step closer to putting this experience behind you.

3. Contact the Authorities

There are many different entities that you should consider contacting in order to report neglect or abuse. A few of the most popular options are:

- The Police
- The Center for Medicare or Medicaid

- Adult Protective Services
- Your State's Ombudsman
- A Lawyer

Neglect and abuse can be crimes. This means that the police should be informed of such actions. You should call the police as soon as you learn of abuse so that the perpetrators can be arrested and prevented from harming other people.

In addition to informing the police of the crime committed against your parent, you can contact adult protective services for assistance. These services can help at risk adults prevent and recover from abuse.

If your parent has Medicare or Medicaid, he or she can contact the Center for Medicare or the Center for Medicaid in order to get help. Those with Medicare and Medicaid enjoy certain rights and privileges, and if any of their rights are violated, one of these services can help.

Each state has ombudsmen that investigate issues in nursing homes in order to protect all residents. An ombudsman is in charge of making changes at the local, state, and even national level to make sure that nursing homes are safe and residents are treated correctly. You can contact your local ombudsman and he or she can investigate the situation and try to bring about change. You can call 1-800-677-1116 to get the number of your local ombudsman.

If you would like to file a lawsuit against those responsible for abuse, it is in your best interest to hire a lawyer. A lawyer can walk you through the process of filing a lawsuit, if this is the direction that you want to go in. A lawyer can also prepare you for the possibility of a criminal case if the abuser is charged and tried, and represent your loved one in court as counsel for the victim.

4. Get Your Parent Out of the Home

Once neglect and abuse have been identified, you need to protect your parent from any future incidents. You should do this by removing your parent from the nursing home where he or she has been abused. If getting your parent out of the home is not an option, or if it will take some time to make this transition, you should protect your parent by taking the following steps:

- Discuss the situation with the Director of Operations or someone else that is in charge of operations.
- Have your parent moved to another wing of the facility.
- Make sure that your parent does not have any contact with the staff member(s) who neglected or abused him or her.
- Get a restraining order against the abuser(s).
- Visit frequently to make sure that your parent has not been abused again.
- Make sure that the police are aware of the situation.

5. Seek Emotional Help

As a victim of neglect and abuse, your parent has been traumatized. He or she needs a way to work through the various emotions that he or she is feeling, including fear, anger, frustration, depression, etc. As soon as possible, you should seek emotional help so that your parent can deal with these emotions, confront what happened to him or her, and move on. Having your parent see a therapist is oftentimes the best way to work through this experience in a healthy and positive way. If your parent is opposed to seeing a therapist, you can contact the Office on Aging or a doctor for alternative treatment. Be sure to monitor your parent's behavior at this difficult time and do what you can to help him or her through it.

6. Write Everything Down

You should help your parent make a record of everything that happened to him or her. While this can be a painful experience for both you and your parent, it is important that your parent writes down what happened as soon as possible. This information will help the police and it will come in handy if you eventually decide to pursue a civil case against the responsible parties. If you would like help with this process, you can ask for the assistance of a police officer. He or she will know what kind of information that your parent needs to write down. A good start when trying to recount the neglect or abuse is to ask your parent the following questions:

- When did the abuse begin?
- How long did the abuse last (was it one incident or multiple incidents?).
- Can you describe the abuse in as much detail as possible?
- Can you describe your injuries in as much detail as possible?
- Did you notice any events or actions that triggered the abuse?
- Do you know of other residents that were also abused?
- Were you abused by one person or more than one person?

- Did you seek help for the abuse, but found that you were ignored?
- Did you tell anyone about the abuse?
- Who abused you?

Gathering this information will help you determine the extent of the abuse, the type of abuse, who is responsible, and more. Another reason to write down everything that happened is to make a record of it for future purposes.

7. Visit a Doctor

Contacting a doctor in the event of abuse is always in your best interest. Whether the abuse was physical, sexual, or emotional, a doctor can identify warning signs of abuse and validate your parent's claims. In most cases, a doctor will want to interview and examine your parent for signs of abuse. Having a doctor confirm the abuse can assist the police in building a case against the perpetrator(s). It can also be used should you and your family decide to file a lawsuit against the nursing home or the staff member(s) who abused your parent.

8. Gather Evidence

Writing down what happened and visiting a doctor are two great first steps in gathering evidence to prove that neglect or abuse took place; however, there are other ways to gather evidence that you should consider in order to help both the police and your family. A few other common ways to gather evidence include:

- Taking photographs

- Taking statements from witnesses and eyewitnesses
- Establishing a history of abuse
- Keeping a paper trail

If your parent is a victim of neglect or physical abuse, there will be physical signs of this abuse, whether that means bruises, broken bones, cuts, poor grooming, etc. Be sure to take pictures of these injuries to document the abuse and provide a physical example of what took place.

If anyone witnessed the neglect or abuse, you should try to get a statement from those people to confirm that neglect or abuse took place. This can include getting an official statement from your parent, a roommate, another staff member, etc.

Oftentimes when abuse takes place, there have been similar incidents that have occurred already. Research the abusers' criminal histories to see if they have been accused of abuse in the past. Also try to learn about specific complaints made to the nursing home about these staff members to show a history of abuse.

You should keep track of any expenses that your parent must pay related to the neglect or abuse. For example, keep a paper trail of:

- Bills for doctor's visits
- Therapy
- Hospital bills
- Medication bills
- Surgery bills

Any expenses related to the abuse should be documented.

9. Hire a Lawyer

You might be wondering if your parent needs a lawyer in this situation. In most cases, the answer is yes. Hiring a lawyer can help your parent understand the civil and criminal processes that his or her abuser(s) will now go through and what may be expected of your parent during this process. To make sure that your parent's rights are protected if he or she is called as a witness, it is important that he or she has legal representation. A lawyer can also answer any questions, handle relevant paperwork, and generally make this process as easy as possible.

10. Decide if You Want to File a Lawsuit

As the victim of abuse, your parent is legally allowed to bring a civil case against his or her abuser(s). One benefit of filing a lawsuit is being compensated for pain and suffering; however, filing a lawsuit is not something that every victim of abuse wants to do. Your parent might decide that the criminal charges brought against the abuser(s) are enough, and that he or she just wants to put this experience in the past as quickly as possible. You should discuss these options with your parent and with a lawyer to determine the best course of action for your situation.

BONUS CONTENT: 10 LEGAL TERMS YOU NEED TO KNOW

If you decide to go ahead with a lawsuit against the parties responsible for your parent's abuse, there are many legal terms that you will have to familiarize yourself with. Here, you can get the basics on 10 of the most important legal terms for you to know at this time. For more assistance, you should contact a lawyer.

1. Defendant

The defendant in a case can be the person being accused of committing a crime, or the defendant in a lawsuit is the person accused of neglect or abuse. This is a term used in both civil and criminal cases, and it means the same thing in both. If a criminal case is brought against your parent's abuser, he or she will be considered the defendant in that case as well.

2. Plaintiff

The plaintiff in a civil case is the party bringing charges against someone else. In this situation, your parent will be the plaintiff of the lawsuit. This term is only used to distinguish your parent's position in the case and does not have any negative connotations.

3. Liability

Liability refers to the party that is legally responsible for the safety of the residents in a nursing home. The person or entity that is legally liable for the safety of a nursing home's residents is the one that will be pursued should neglect or abuse take place. In some cases, the person that committed the neglect or abuse will be held liable. In other situations, the nursing home owners might also be held liable for the actions of their employees.

4. Duty/Breach of Duty

In order for neglect or abuse to take place, two things must be proven. First, that the abuser (or the defendant in the case) had a duty to your parent. Second, that the defendant breached this duty by causing your parent harm. You can prove that the employee had a duty to care for your parent because he or she was a resident of the nursing home. The employee did not fulfill this duty because he or she neglected or abused your parent.

5. Breach of Contract

A breach of contract is similar to breach of duty. If you can prove that breach of contract occurred, you can probably also prove that breach of duty occurred.

Most nursing homes ask nurses and other staff members to sign a contract promising to care for all residents to the best of their abilities. If an employee fails to do this by neglecting or abusing a resident, breach of contract will take place. This can be one factor in a lawsuit against the liable party.

6. Deposition

If you are involved in a lawsuit against someone who has neglected or abused your parent, chances are that depositions will take place. Your parent's lawyer will most likely depose the defendant in the case as well as other staff members, the Director of Operations, and other relevant people. A deposition is a piece of sworn evidence that will try to make your case stronger. Depositions occur under oath, meaning that if you lie during a deposition, you could be charged with perjury. This means that when your parent's lawyer deposes someone, you can collect evidence against the defendant in the case in order to make your argument stronger.

In some cases, the defendant's lawyer will depose your parent. Your parent must give testimony at a deposition if he or she is deposed, but there is no need for your parent to be nervous about giving a deposition. His or her lawyer will be present and will make sure that the questions are appropriate. So long as your parent answers honestly or to the best of his or her ability, there shouldn't be any issues.

7. Pretrial Period/Hearing

Before a trial takes place, there will be a pretrial period in which both parties can gather evidence, file motions, and prepare their arguments. At the end of this period is a pretrial hearing in which both parties and their lawyers will meet with a judge to attempt to resolve any legal issues before the actual trial begins. This ensures that both parties are on the same page and that they are prepared for trial.

8. Settlement

In many civil cases, one party or both parties will attempt to settle the case before it goes to trial. There are many different reasons to settle the case. Maybe you realize that your case is not as strong as you initially thought it was. Maybe the nursing home wants to avoid the risk of trial and establish a compromise instead. Whatever the reason, either party may propose a settlement before the case goes to trial. In most cases, the plaintiff is the one that proposes a settlement, but either party may try to settle the case before it goes to trial. If a settlement is reached, trial will be avoided. If both parties cannot come to an agreement, the case will proceed to trial.

9. Compensation

One of the main purposes of filing a lawsuit against an abuser is to receive compensation for the pain and suffering that your parent has experienced. Compensation can be provided for:

- Any bills associated with the neglect or abuse (hospital bills, medication, medical equipment, etc.)
- Money or property that was stolen
- Pain
- Suffering

These are the main categories that compensation will be provided for. A judge or jury will determine compensation for each case based on your parent's specific situation.

10. Statute of Limitations

In each state, there is a certain amount of time that a victim has to file a lawsuit against the at-fault party. This time period is known as the statute of limitations. Once the statute of limitations passes, your parent will no longer have the right to file a lawsuit against his or her abuser. The statute of limitations is different in each state, but regardless of the time period that you have, It is always best to be proactive and begin building your case as soon as possible.

CONCLUSION

We hope that you have found this book helpful in your attempt to keep your parent safe from neglect and abuse.

If, through the warning signs mentioned in this book, you realize that your parent has been neglected or abused in his or her nursing home, you should take action immediately. When you contact us, we can answer your specific questions and help you determine the next step to take in your situation.

We understand that this is a difficult time for you, and we would like to help in any way that we can. Please contact us for further assistance at 203-925-9200.

Made in the USA
Monee, IL
04 November 2026

67386431R10059